The Peninsula Surprise

by Juanita Havill
illustrated by Paul Lackner

Scott Foresman

Editorial Offices: Glenview, Illinois • New York, New York
Sales Offices: Reading, Massachusetts • Duluth, Georgia
Glenview, Illinois • Carrollton, Texas • Menlo Park, California

"Wait for Rojo!" Jesse shouted. He held open the car door for his dog. Rojo jumped into the car.

Papa started the car and drove Mama, Carlos, Linda, Jesse, and Rojo out of the city. They crossed the Golden Gate Bridge and headed up the coast to a popular beach.

"Please, Papa, can we go farther away to a more deserted place?" Jesse asked.

"Not too far, Papa," Linda complained. "If we go out too far, there won't be anyone there."

"You mean *boys*," Carlos teased his sister.

Papa glanced at his watch. "We have plenty of time. Let's find a quiet cove." He winked at Jesse in the rearview mirror. "Jesse is in the mood for adventure."

"I'm always in the mood for adventure," Jesse said. He loved to explore new places.

They came to a small cove, drove down a gravel road, and parked near the beach along the cove. It was cloudy and turning chilly when the family unloaded the car.

"Hey, Jesse, do you want to play catch?" Papa said.

"No, I'm going to explore first," Jesse replied.

"Don't go by yourself," Mama said. "Carlos, keep an eye on your brother."

Jesse rolled his eyes. He didn't need a baby-sitter. But he knew better than to question his mother.

Jesse chased after Rojo along the rocky shore. Carlos followed behind them. The beach was smooth and sandy in some places and stretched around the shore of the cove. In other places there were rocks littering the wet, gray sand. Jesse had to dodge them and even jump over some big rocks that jutted out of the sand. Waves from the ocean splashed against half-submerged rocks not far from shore.

"Rojo, slow down. You're moving too fast," called Carlos loudly.

Rojo didn't stop or slow down. He barked at the waves and chased seagulls. When the graceful white birds lifted up in flight over the cove, Rojo jumped up to catch them.

Rojo looked as if he were trying to fly. Jesse smiled at the thought.

Jesse and Carlos followed Rojo to a large formation of rocks that led to a wide strip of land. They climbed up on a rock. Jesse could see that the land jutted out into the ocean. It was a small peninsula. On one side of the peninsula was the cove where they had arrived. On the other side Jesse could see a smaller cove with no sand beach at all—just rocks and boulders. Some of the rocks were submerged. Others jutted unevenly out of the water.

Jesse jumped down from the boulder and set off to explore the peninsula with Rojo. Carlos was soon behind him.

Scrubby bushes, rocks, and a few trees surrounded them. Jesse was soon out in front with Rojo dashing off on little side trips, then running back to check on him. Suddenly, Carlos saw a thin pole sticking up from the water behind some rocks.

"Jesse," Carlos called, and headed down the slope toward the rocky cove to investigate. Jesse followed his brother. All he could think was that a storm had blown a sailboat against the rocks.

The boys edged out on the rocks and discovered that the sailboat was not completely submerged. It had taken on water but was wedged between rocks that kept it from sinking. Carlos crawled onto the deck to explore and told Jesse to wait on the rocks.

Carlos opened a compartment and saw a couple of granola bars, a flashlight, a lighter, and a map. There were no names, nothing to tell him about the owner. Jesse wanted to run right back and tell Papa. But the wind picked up and a cold rain began to fall.

The boys headed inland to look for shelter. They crawled into a shallow cave underneath a boulder. Rojo, soggy and full of wet sand, sat panting beside them.

Rain poured around them and flowed in streams down the rocky slopes to the cove below. Jesse knew his family would be worried, but what could he do? He figured they had run to the car to sit out the storm. At least he was with Carlos.

It rained a long time. When it finally stopped raining, the boys and Rojo crawled out. Jesse wanted to go back to investigate the boat, but Carlos told him they had to get back to the car.

"Rojo, let's go." Jesse zipped his jacket up to his neck to protect him from the chilly wind. Carlos led the way.

They reached the stand of boulders leading to the other beach. Jesse gasped when he saw that the rocks were now submerged. The tide had come in and raised the water level above the rocks. Soon only the tops of the largest boulders would stick out of the water. The tide had cut the peninsula off from the mainland and had turned it into an island.

The water was too deep to wade and too cold to swim. It was too dangerous to jump across the boulders. Maybe Rojo could. Jesse wasn't sure what to do. If he and Carlos had to stay there all night until the tide went out, he wanted Rojo to be with them. Besides, how could he be sure that Rojo would find his family? What if they had driven up the coast to look for him and his brother? Rojo would be all alone.

"It looks as if we'll have to wait here for the tide to go out," said Carlos. "Go look for twigs and leaves so that I can make a fire."

Carlos went back to the sailboat, opened the compartment, and took out the flashlight, lighter, and granola bars. He tried to switch on the flashlight. The batteries were dead. He clicked the lighter and a weak flame rose up. He put the flashlight back and set off for the other side of the peninsula with the lighter and the snack food.

Jesse gathered any dry twigs and leaves he could find under rocks or trees. By the time he got back to Carlos, it was dark enough for a fire to be visible.

The boys drank some water from the bottle in Jesse's pack and opened a granola bar to take a few nibbles.

It was dark now. Jesse looked for lights along the shore. Yes! A car headed down the shore toward the peninsula. But it was turning around. Its red tail lights blinked at him.

Carlos was trying to build a fire. He only had enough sticks for a small one. Maybe their parents had called the Coast Guard, who would see the fire from their patrol boat.

Carlos made a loose pile of sticks and set the granola wrapper underneath it. He lit the wrapper with the lighter. Once it started burning, the small twigs burst into flame. The fire sputtered and Carlos blew gently on the flames until they finally blazed up.

Rojo crouched away from the fire, but Jesse rubbed his hands and felt the welcome warmth. He peered out into the darkness.

"Please let someone see the fire," he said. Then he remembered how he had been the one who wanted to go to a deserted spot where there wouldn't be so many people.

"I'm glad Mama made you come with me," Jesse told Carlos. Carlos smiled back at his younger brother.

Raindrops began to fall. The boys watched the fire sputter and curls of smoke rise up. It rained harder and the fire finally died out. There was nothing left to do but seek shelter and wait until morning.

Carlos found dry ground under a rocky overhang and pulled Jesse and Rojo close to him. It was dark and scary, but Jesse tried to stay calm.

Carlos comforted him. "It's totally safe. There's nothing to worry about." But it took Jesse a long time to fall asleep.

Jesse woke with a start when Rojo poked his cold wet nose against his cheek. Carlos was already awake. Jesse got up and stretched stiffly. They headed for the boulder bridge. The tide had gone out, and now they could cross from the peninsula to the mainland.

Jesse and Carlos started running up the beach, ahead of Rojo this time. Jesse looked for the car, but when he and Carlos got to the place where he was sure they had left it, he didn't see it.

"It looks as if we're going to have a long walk, Carlos," he said.

The boys started to walk up the winding gravel road that led to the highway above. They rounded a curve in the road then whooped and jumped up in the air.

There was the car, with Papa, Mama, and Linda sleeping in it.

Jesse knocked on the window and Papa sat up. "They're back!" he shouted.

Everyone got out and took turns hugging the boys. Their parents scolded the boys a little and asked them what had happened.

"We called the police," Mama said.

"And the Coast Guard," Linda said.

"We had quite a rainstorm, but we didn't want to leave. So we camped in the car until morning," Papa said.

Jesse told them about the tide and how Carlos had tried to make a fire. Then he told them about the boat. "May we go back now? I want to show you. Maybe we can find out where it's from."

"First, we need to tell the people who are looking for you that we found you," said Mama.

"We'll have some breakfast in the town up ahead," Papa said. "On the way back we'll stop and investigate this boat you found."

"Aren't you glad I asked Carlos to go with you?" Mama said to Jesse.

Jesse looked over at his older brother. Carlos winked back. As usual, Mama was right.